My State
VIRGINIA

By Christina Earley

TABLE OF CONTENTS

A Crabtree Seedlings Book

Crabtree Publishing
crabtreebooks.com

School-to-Home Support for Caregivers and Teachers

This book helps children grow by letting them practice reading. Here are a few guiding questions to help the reader build his or her comprehension skills. Possible answers appear in red.

Before Reading:

- What do I know about Virginia?
    - *I know that Virginia is a state.*
    - *I know that Virginia has a lot of beaches.*

- What do I want to learn about Virginia?
    - *I want to learn which famous people were born in Virginia.*
    - *I want to learn what the state flag looks like.*

During Reading:

- What have I learned so far?
    - *I have learned that Richmond is the state capital of Virginia.*
    - *I have learned that Williamsburg was once the capital of Virginia.*

- I wonder why...
    - *I wonder why the state flower is the flowering dogwood.*
    - *I wonder why the first peanuts grown in the U.S. were grown in Virginia.*

After Reading:

- What did I learn about Virginia?
    - *I have learned that the Natural Bridge is 215 feet (66 m) high.*
    - *I have learned that the state bird is the northern cardinal.*

- Read the book again and look for the glossary words.
    - *I see the word **capital** on page 6, and the word **patriotic** on page 14. The other glossary words are found on pages 22 and 23.*

VIRGINIA

I live in Alexandria. My city was **founded** in 1749!

The Old Town Farmers' Market has been held in Alexandria for more than 260 years. George Washington sold his **produce** here!

Virginia is in the eastern United States. The **capital** is Richmond.

Fun Fact: Virginia Beach is the largest city in Virginia.

The state bird is the northern cardinal.

The flowering dogwood is the state flower.

We grow a lot of peanuts in Virginia. Virginia peanuts are a delicious snack.

Fun Fact: The first peanuts grown in the U.S. were grown in Virginia.

My state flag is blue. The state **seal** is in the middle.

I like to go surfing at Croatan Beach.

Colonial Williamsburg is a living-history museum. Hearing the march of the **fifes** and drums makes me feel **patriotic**.

Fun Fact: Williamsburg was once the capital of Virginia.

I like to explore Luray Caverns. They are the largest caverns in the eastern U.S.

The Great Channels is my favorite place to go hiking.

Actress Sandra Bullock was born in Virginia. Olympic champion gymnast Gabby Douglas was also born in Virginia.

Fun Fact: President George Washington was born in Westmoreland County, Virginia.

I love to ride the roller coasters at Busch Gardens.

I like to visit Natural Bridge State Park. The Natural Bridge is 215 feet (66 m) high!

Glossary

capital (cap-ih-tuhl): The city or town where the government of a country, state, or province is located

fife (fahyf): A small flute commonly used in military bands

founded (found-ed): Created or set up

patriotic (pay-tree-ot-ik): Having great love for your country

produce (proh-doos): Fresh fruits and vegetables

seal (seel): A special design that is used on important papers and other items

Index

About the Author

Christina Earley lives in sunny South Florida with her husband and son. She enjoys traveling around the United States and learning about different historical places. Her hobbies include hiking, yoga, and baking.

Written by: Christina Earley
Designed and Illustrated by: Bobbie Houser
Series Development: James Earley
Proofreader: Melissa Boyce
Educational Consultant: Marie Lemke M.Ed.

Photographs:
Alamy: Charles O. Cecil: p. 5, 23; Emanuel Tanjala: p. 17; James Kirkikis: p. 20
Shutterstock: Bob Pool: cover; Jon Marc Lyttle: p. 3; Jon Bilous: p. 4, 23; Volina: p. 6, 22; Sherry V Smith: p. 7; Bonnie Taylor Barry: p. 8; PAUL ATKINSON: p. 9; Ricardo Ninin: p. 10-11; dinosmichail: p. 11; railway fx: p. 12, 23; Felix Mizioznikov: p. 13; Kim Kelley-Wagner: p. 14, 22; Daniel Reiner: p. 14-15, 23; jgorzynik: p. 16, 22; Fred Duval: p. 18 left; Rena Schild: p. 18 right; Everett Collection: p. 19; Zack Frank: p. 21

Crabtree Publishing

crabtreebooks.com 800-387-7650

Printed in the U.S.A./072023/CG20230214

Published in Canada
Crabtree Publishing
616 Welland Avenue
St. Catharines, Ontario
L2M 5V6

Published in the United States
Crabtree Publishing
347 Fifth Avenue
Suite 1402-145
New York, New York, 10016

Library and Archives Canada Cataloguing in Publication
Available at Library and Archives Canada

Library of Congress Cataloging-in-Publication Data
Available at the Library of Congress

Hardcover: 978-1-0398-0539-2
Paperback: 978-1-0398-0571-2
Ebook (pdf): 978-1-0398-0635-1
Epub: 978-1-0398-0603-0